HOW TO EXPERIENCE THE SUPERNATURAL POWER OF FASTING AND PRAYER

FRANCESCO BASILE

Author: Doctor **Francesco Basile**

Editing and proofreading
Davide Duranti

First edition October 2018

Biblical quotes, unless otherwise indicated, are taken from:
New International Version

INDEX

To you reader

Thank you for purchasing this powerful book,
I am sure that after studying your life
will never be the same.

I also encourage you to stay connected with us
to keep up to date with the latest news,
free materials and lectures.

Go immediately to www.francescobasile.tv

INTRODUCTION

Prayer and fasting are two of the most effective weapons in the arsenal of a believer! I thank God, I have learned how to grow up and make progress in my Christian walk. There is no promotion that will ever raise us to a level where we can say that we have no further need for prayer and fasting.

The greater the commitment and dedication to prayer and fasting, the more we progress in the spiritual realm and the higher the degree of authority in the believers' life. Jesus never said "If" you fast, nor "if" you pray, but His words were: "When you pray... and When you fast..." In believers' life, there has to be a "when" devoted to prayer and fasting.

Scripture gives us several instances of prayer and fasting:

- Paul didn't eat anything for three days and, after the fasting period, recovered his sight (*Acts* 9);
- Daniel ate no delicacies for 21 days and received his breakthrough (*Daniel* 10:2);
- Ester completed three days of complete fasting for the liberation of her people and succeeded (*Esther* 9);
- Anna, the prophetess, ministered to the Lord in the Temple with prayers and fasting (*Luke* 2:37);
- the fervent prayers of the church in Acts saw the release of angelic provision and Peter released from jail (*Acts* 12);
- John the Baptist made fasting his way of life: he fed on honey and wild locusts.

Scripture is full of examples of consecration to God. That's something very personal. You have to find the right combination between God and you, a rhythm that finds confirmation in your heart.

If you want to start fasting, I suggest you do it in moderation. Begin by skipping a meal, and estimate your day without ignoring physical issues nor medical treatments. Everything needs to be done wisely, respecting your body.

There's not a right or wrong way to fast, but there's the fasting that works for you, the most suitable between God and you! For those not used to it, it's often arduous. On the other hand, when God trains us, the Holy Spirit guides us, giving us strength from above to do what He asks us. The Holy Spirit gives us the grace to do what God asks us to do. Jesus taught and showed us the importance of prayer and fasting through His personal example.

His public ministry began with forty days of fasting:

> *Jesus, full of the Holy Spirit, left the Jordan and was led by the Spirit into the wilderness, where for forty days he was tempted by the devil. He ate nothing during those days, and at the end of them he was hungry.*
> **Luke 4:1-2**

In these verses, we see Jesus entering His ministry. John the Baptist just baptized Him and immediately, the Holy Spirit led Him into the desert on a fast. When considering these verses, some questions came to my mind:

- Why did Jesus have to go into the desert to fast?

-   What was the Holy Spirit leading Jesus to fast from?

Fasting isn't just to abstain from some meals or foods: it's a form of prayer, a way to consecrate your time to God. I think that the Holy Spirit led Jesus into the desert to make Him fast from His previous way of life, from His facilities. In other words, that time in the desert separated Him from all that could have distracted Him from giving his full attention to God, and all that God wanted to convey to Him.

Fasting separates you from everyday life to lead you in a set-apart time to God, a time dedicated only to Him. Taking such a step means saying to God: "Lord, you're more important than everything: than food, than my plans, than my friends, than my possessions!"

> ***Fasting separates you from everyday life
> to lead you in a set-apart time with God,
> a time dedicated only to Him.***

Fasting is a special alone-time with God in which you devote yourself exclusively to Him, praying and studying His Word. I firmly believe that fasting is one of the highest forms of prayer to which the Holy Spirit sooner or later wants to lead every child of God!

The Word says:

> *...he jealously longs for the spirit he has caused to dwell in us*

> ***James 4:5***

Sometimes the fasting God asks you is needed to restore the intimacy between the two of you, annulling all the other things that are becoming too important for you. God wants to spend time with you, earnestly desires to have a supernatural encounter with you, but you have to give Him the central position in your life and plans.

When you fast, your fleshly side loses strength, making your body more and more a tool for God's purpose - not yours. Then, every cell of your body will learn to magnify God!

Jesus Christ the Lord, beloved Son of God Who came on earth and took the form of a man to redeem the lost and the sin-corrupted humankind, didn't suffer to the point of shedding blood and dying on the cross only to forgive our sins.

From the beginning, God the Father, God the Son, and God the Holy Ghost desired to pour into men and women the **"VITALITY OF GOD,"** His breath of life, so that humans, united with God, could walk in the **SUPERNATURAL POWER** of the heaven. God doesn't want you to be in heaven only for a day; He longs to pour as of now heaven into you! When Jesus Christ the Lord rose again on the third day by the work of the Holy Spirit, that act of supremacy over death, sin, and the enemy, enabled all who believed in Him and received His Spirit in their hearts to potentially become supernatural tools for God!

Today the same Spirit Who raised Christ from the dead abides in our hearts to unleash the same SUPERNATURAL POWER that operated in the lives of Jesus' disciples – talked about in the Book of Acts and now is available to us.

Start on this journey today, discovering the SUPERNATURAL POWER OF FASTING AND PRAYER that is available to you!

There's a new spiritual dimension available for those who hunger for more of God in their lives.

WE CAN DEFINE PRAYER IN THREE
WORDS: STAYING WITH GOD.
-Francesco Basile

CHAPTER 1
PRAYER AS A WAY OF LIFE

Without a revelation about prayer, my life wouldn't have been the same. For many, praying is a duty, a moment to complain before God or make a list of needs. For me, prayer is to have access, be listened to, and to have friendship with the sweetest and most friendly person I've ever met. We can define prayer in three words: Staying with God. In five: Having intimacy with the Lord. In nine words: God so loves me that He listens to me.

Let's have a look at the way of life and the way that Jesus prayed:

> *When all the people were being baptized, Jesus was baptized too.* **And as he was praying, heaven was opened** *and the Holy Spirit descended on him in bodily form like a dove. And a voice came from heaven: "You are my Son, whom I love; with you I am well pleased."*
> **Luke 3:21-22**

Heaven was opened over Jesus as He was praying. He knew Father's voice well because prayer is more than talking to God: it's listening to what He has to tell us. His words change our existence. That's why, in the multitude of our undertakings, we should take time daily to stay with God.

*At daybreak, **Jesus went out to a solitary place**. The people were looking for him and when they came to where he was, they tried to keep him from leaving them.*
Luke 4:42

There was a time I went to the mountains to pray. I spent several hours walking with God, surrounded by greenery. While I was having this private moment with Him, the Lord spoke to my heart, saying: "Francesco, every one of my children needs to learn to spend time alone with me: that's a priority." Look at Jesus' lifestyle. We immediately notice that He used to spend a lot of time in intense prayer when He had to make decisions that would have changed and affected many lives.

*One of those days Jesus went out to a mountainside to pray, and **spent the night** praying to God. When morning came, he called his disciples to him and chose twelve of them, whom he also designated apostles:*
Luke 6:12-13

Jesus used to pray before any crucial choice - and He prayed before calling on His disciples too. That choice meant we could have access to the Gospels we have written today. Never underestimate what God can reveal to you in prayer because it could change history for generations to come.

Sometimes, as we pray, we experience a slice of heaven on earth:

About eight days after Jesus said this, he took Peter, John and James with him and went up onto a mountain to pray. As he was praying, the appearance of his face changed, and his clothes became as bright as a flash of lightning.

Luke 9:28-29

Prayer **BRINGS INTO EVIDENCE OUR TRUE NATURE**, prayer brings out what God has put in us, and removes the shell that often limits us. Sometimes Jesus devoted whole nights to prayer. Why at night? Because the night time is silent and, in that silence, it's easier to remain in a listening mode, emptying our minds from

1. **thoughts**
2. **pressures**
3. **concerns**

Thoughts crowd your mind, pressures and deadlines blur your sight, worries distract you from the biggest blessing Jesus won for us with His death, burial, and resurrection: open access to the throne of grace.

God is waiting for you. Don't hesitate any longer. Pick a place, some time, and leave outside every distraction. Your Heavenly Father wants to abide with you.

GOD WANTS ALL OF YOU,
NOT ONLY SOME PARTS
- Francesco Basile

CHAPTER 2
SETTING OURSELVES
APART WITH THE
HOLY SPIRIT

God made countless treasures available for us in the spiritual realm. In God's kingdom, we find all we need. We can experience life on earth with the strength, the resources, and the possibilities of heaven.

How? By beginning with setting ourselves apart for the Lord.

In Luke 5, Jesus says to Levi: " 'Follow me,' […] and Levi got up, left everything […]"

> *Now in the church at Antioch there were prophets and teachers: Barnabas, Simeon called Niger, Lucius of Cyrene, Manaen (who had been brought up with Herod the tetrarch) and Saul. While they were worshiping the Lord and fasting, the Holy Spirit said, "Set apart for me Barnabas and Saul for the work to which I have called them." So after they had fasted and prayed, they placed their hands on them and sent them off. The two of them, sent on their way by the Holy*

*Spirit, went down to Seleucia and sailed from
there to Cyprus.*
Acts 13:1-4

The apostle Paul, first called Saul, set himself apart for the Lord
through preparation that lasted over 13 years. He left behind all
that he had accomplished as Saul (admirable and desired personality) to enter what God had prepared for him as Paul (a man of hu-
mility and servitude).

Setting ourselves apart, sanctifying ourselves for the Lord, is
WHAT WE DO FOR HIM, for the Holy One.

Sanctification is a relationship, not a job. You're not an employee.
All that God gives you isn't governed by a contract. You are a child
who lives 100% for a purpose.

SETTING APART MEANS THE FOLLOWING:

1. **To give God all that we are.**
   Jesus didn't take one fish and one loaf of bread, but he took
   two fishes and five loaves. He wants all of you, not only
   some parts of your life. Many want to be used by God for
   the multitudes, but few of them are willing to be broken
   into 5000 small pieces.

2. **To give God what we have.**
   We need to learn to set ourselves apart for the Lord, and
   give into His hands what is precious to us, this will enable us
   to enter what is "precious for God". All that we have is like
   a seed we plant in God, and with Him, over time, we will
   have a good harvest.

3. **To give God control of our lives.**

Letting things go, not letting the things in your life control you.

Peter renounced his pride, his boat, his personality.

Barnabas left Antioch to go on a mission with Paul in unknown lands.

Timothy chose to be persecuted for the sake of the Gospel rather than pursuing his own passions.

Moses left behind the wealth of Egy pt and also all his inheritances.

Abraham left his comfort zone, his homeland, his family.

Jesus left His glory at the right hand of the Father for over 33 years.

Giving up. Setting apart. Going. This is what it means to be set apart for God.

3 KEYS TO A SET-APART LIFE IN PRAYER

1. **PUT PRAYER FIRST**

> *At each and every sunrise, I will give you every part of me; I will lay down on your altar any thought, hope, and dream of my heart. I will expose and submit every molecule of my life between earth and heaven to your fire, waiting for your fire that only you can give me by your Spirit [...]*

> **Psalm 5:2-3 (TPT - paraphrase)**

> **God deserves our best time, our first fruits, and our best words.**

Scripture often speaks about praying in the early morning, in the quiet dawn, or in the silence of the night. Prayer finds its best expression in the first light of the day, before the concerns of the day crowd our minds, and the phone or our schedules catch our attention.

Not everyone can do it, nor is that necessarily the best moment for praying, but there's something glorious and powerful about beginning the day in the presence of the Lord. God said to Moses:

> *Be ready in the morning, and then come up on Mount Sinai. Present yourself to me there on top of the mountain. No one is to come with you or be seen anywhere on the mountain; not even the flocks and herds may graze in front of the mountain.*
>
> **Exodus 34:2-3**

We schedule our day, set our priorities, and put the things that are most important to us early in the morning. God deserves our best time, our first fruits, and our best words. I encourage you by saying, "Be ready tomorrow morning."

2. MAKE HIS PRESENCE YOUR FIRST GOAL

> *Yet the news about him spread all the more, so that crowds of people came to hear him and to be healed of their sicknesses. But Jesus often withdrew to lonely places and prayed.*
>
> **Luke 5:15-16**

In His earthly life, Jesus taught that prayer was always a privilege for Him. All those who got in touch with Him were astounded by His relationship with the Father. Scripture clearly teaches that praying is one of the highest privileges for every child of God. The Word states that *"Therefore, brothers and sisters, since we have confidence to enter the Most Holy Place by the blood of Jesus, by a new and living way opened for us" (Hebrews 10:19-20)*

Having access to prayer depends not on the role one has in the church: it's a privilege the Lord directly bestows on any of us. It depends not on the experience one has or hasn't had with Him, because you become part of God's family immediately after having said "Yes" to Jesus. Nobody, not even the devil himself, can hinder or deny your legitimacy, because Jesus chose to give you the right to be His child. Let's enter into prayer today and enjoy this amazing fellowship with God!

3. **GIVE PRAYER TIME**

> *But those who hope in the Lord will renew their strength. They will soar on wings like eagles; they will run and not grow weary, they will walk and not be faint.*
> **Isaiah 40:31**

The most intimate prayer is often wordless: it consists of a time entirely spent in fellowship with God, not only to ask or claim something. It's a time when we learn to wait and listen to what our God and Father wants to tell us.

Prayer will take you to high peaks with God.

We will know how to pray when we've learned that words aren't always needed, when spending time with Him is enough. True fellowship with God is also remaining silent in His presence.

Be still before the Lord and wait patiently for him [...]
Psalm 37:7

The most intense moments of closeness with God aren't those when we talk or are trying to convey something: the most unforgettable instanances in His presence are those when words become superfluous. We have the most profound moments of fellowship when His presence becomes our everything.

Prayer will take you to the high mountain peaks with God.

NOTES

FAITH IS NOT THE ABSENCE OF DIF-
FICULTIES, BUT IT IS THE WAY OUT
OF EVERY DIFFICULTY.

- Francesco Basile

CHAPTER 3
DEEPER WITH GOD
PART I

Some years ago, I was in London for a time of rest and searching after the mind of the Lord. It was then that the Holy Spirit revealed to me the four keys of prayer that I'm going to share with you now.

> *Be ready in the morning, and then come up on Mount Sinai. Present yourself to me there on top of the mountain. No one is to come with you or be seen anywhere on the mountain; not even the flocks and herds may graze in front of the mountain.*
> **Exodus 34:2-3**

The first key I have received from that verse is: GET UP.

God doesn't necessarily ask you to get up early, but He, no doubt, calls you to get up earlier: before your day starts and before the daily concerns start filling your mind. Sometimes this is the hardest thing to do because your mind is filled with thoughts even before you get up, so you have tremendous interior chaos in your soul (feelings, thoughts, emotions), you however, need quiet and silence in these moments.

Give God the first place, and all the remaining will go to the right place!

Why should we pray in the early morning? Because we often set the temperature of our day from the start of our day! I have realized that when I stop praying and spending time with the Lord, I'm setting my day's weather.

Everyone has a "bad day" sooner or later. Nothing goes right; the easy things seem hard, and everything is against you. Suddenly you think: this morning I didn't pray!

There are two opposite kinds of people: the thermometers and the thermostats. Those who never spend time with the Lord are in the thermometer group. They passively live their lives. They feel the temperature of their surroundings; they can even sense the difference between different days, but they don't have the strength to do anything to change it.

On the other hand, those who pray and spend time before the Lord are the thermostats!

What's the difference between a thermometer and a thermostat? The first can only measure the temperature; the latter can change it. The thermometer watches the temperature, but the thermostat sets it.

When you pray in the morning, you are active, not passive. You are taking a stand, and you can choose if you want to live by taking the day as it comes or by knowing that God will be with you in every moment to show you His glory! You can either live under the influence of the circumstances or see your day changed by God's Spirit Who moves on your behalf, knowing that God will make everything go to the right place and that the doors which were closed will be opened. I want to start my day in the name of Jesus by praying!

I want to be a thermostat, to turn up the heat, and change the circumstances.

> *You can choose if you want to live*
> *by taking the day as it comes or by knowing*
> *that God will be with you in every moment*
> *to show you His glory!*

Unbelief believes what it sees; faith sees what it believes!
A man of faith, of prayer, who sets the day's temperature from the morning remains unshaken in the face of difficult circumstances. He challenges life with the strength of prayer and the power of faith! If you want to see your circumstances changed, don't ask me to pray for you, but take your stand in prayer!

Prayer doesn't work just because you know it works; prayer works because you make it work!
We may not have seen the outcomes or answers to our biggest prayers, because we haven't prayed these prayers yet.

> *At each and every sunrise, I will give you every part of me; I will lay down on your altar any thought, hope, and dream of my heart. I will expose and submit every molecule of my life between earth and heaven to your fire, waiting for your fire that only you can give me by your Spirit [...]*
> **Psalm 5:2-3 (TPT - paraphrase)**

The Psalmist wrote that prayer and dedicated it to God, saying: "At each and every sunrise [...] I will [...] submit [...] to your fire

[...]" Champions daily do what ordinary people do only occasionally!

The Bible says: "At each and every sunrise, I will give you every part of me."

Oh, how many times I wake up in the morning having a thousand thoughts, ambitions and dreams and I get lost in focus to these. Sometimes you may miss your morning meeting with Him, don't fear, because He surely will not change His mind about you.

That's grace!

Champions daily do what ordinary people do only occasionally!

God doesn't move because you pray, but He moves because Jesus has already prayed for you. **Your prayer doesn't make God move towards you, but it makes you move towards Him.**

God doesn't stand still; we are the ones standing still. We are the ones who have to move towards God and look for Him.
The Word goes on saying: "I will lay down on your altar any thought, hope, and dream of my heart [...] waiting for your fire." What does fire do? It purifies.

Often many of our thoughts, ambitions, and dreams have to pass through fire because they don't come from God - they come from us! All that the fire purifies, is what remains and that which remains is what comes from God!

Do you want to know how to distinguish when a project comes from God?

Pass it through the test of fire, the test of prayer! When you still feel peace and victory after having prayed over that project, that idea, and that ambition, then you know that it comes from God.

When we have a project or desire to do something, we often look for encouragement and assurance that the project will succeed from someone important to us.

Nonetheless, God is not asking you to look for confirmation in the words of those around you. He is asking you to pray with Him. He is asking you to talk to Him, to lay down your dreams, projects, ambitions, and talents before Him, and to receive the fire that comes from Him! Don't look for testimonials nor confirmations from people.

Prayer is not made only by questions and answers.
Sometimes it is just staying with God.

"I will expose and submit every molecule of my life [...]"

Sometimes certain situations bodily, mentally, and practically in circumstances of life need to pass through the fire one molecule after another because God's fire brings light when it enters!

I love teaching about prayer because I'm sure that it has changed and is changing my life.
Everything you receive in prayer, all that God puts within your heart as you pray, has already passed the test of fire. All heavenly

things are stronger than anything that comes from the earthly realm!

The best moment for prayer is in the morning. I'm not saying that there are no other moments to pray, but we are fresh and fully rested in the morning, still free from the hectic pace of the day, schedules, and concerns. In the morning, your mind is clear, and therefore every part of you can focus on God. Give God the best of yourself, not when you are feeling tired.

Sometimes we want God to talk to us in our way when we want - often when we have lots of other things to do - as if He should serve us. God is not at our service, He doesn't respond to sentences like: "Lord, speak to me, speak to me now."

You will not always have an answer. **PRAYER** is not made only questions and answers. Sometimes it means just "being with God".

How bad a relationship between husband and wife would be if it were based only on **asking** and **demanding**. When you're in a marriage relationship, sometimes just being close to your spouse is enough; you feel good together, even without doing anything, sometimes even without saying a word. These are the most uplifting moments!

In prayer, you don't necessarily need a lot of words, but you do need your heart!

Many people don't see divine outcomes in their lives only because they don't spend time with God! He doesn't call you to do things for Him, because He doesn't need laborers or robots. He doesn't call you to obey Him as if He were a dictator: He wants you to do things **with** Him!

He doesn't call you a laborer, but He calls you a child!

I sometimes hear young people in my church complaining that they are tired or have had a bad day. I always try to encourage them by saying: "Postpone tiredness to later. Now you are here. Give God all you have: your heart, care and concerns. You may not be able to do anything about your problem, but God can! He can overturn every one of your problems and situations while you are here!" You don't know what God may do for you while you are taking care of His work; that's why I encourage you to give Him the early morning hours!

When God becomes a priority for you, you become a priority for God! *When you put God first, everything else will fall into place!*

Sometimes we try to use prayer to fix the damage we have already done. We use prayer as a remedy and then we complain to God when we don't see the outcomes.

While traveling to different churches, where people asked me to pray for them, demanding that God would fix five years of mistakes in five minutes of prayer. They expect God to remedy five years of disobedience in five minutes of obedience. My friends, God longs for you to go back to a path of obedience and to bow down before Him again, not only for Him to fix things, but often times it's simply to learn to give priority to what He wants!

You will be able to see something different in your life when you start loving intimacy with God, even if He doesn't answer your prayer or doesn't fix things. When you learn to praise Him for who

He is and not just for what He does! That will make all the difference!

***You will be able to see something different
in your life when you start loving staying with God!***

God is very interested in you, not only to bless you, but to transform and change you into someone who will be a blessing.
If you only ask God to bless you, you are only interested in the blessing and this is because you have not yet matured!

When I don't buy my son something he wants, my son starts crying because he's a baby; he throws himself on the ground and screams because he has not yet understood my character. Spiritual babies, who kick, scream and cry before God, thinking that He doesn't want to give them something, have not yet known His heart! The Lord says that He wants to grant us the things we need, even before we ask Him, because He already knows what we need!

A life surrendered in God's presence, leads to a new way to live life. Answers to prayers will arrive even before you have time to say them. You will live a life of abundance; doors that previously were closed will open before you; God will send angels to help assist you.

***Don't spend too much time continuously talking to Him
about your problems, because He already knows about
these.***

***Prayer doesn't work because you know prayer works, but
only when you actually pray.***

Amazed by the way God was using him, pastor Billy Joe Daugherty asked pastor Oral Roberts how many hours he prayed. After a few moments of silence, Roberts answered: *"24 hours a day"* and then went on to say: *"Real prayer is not speaking but always listening."*

Prayer is listening. Time spent with God in private and it will give you the ability to identify His voice in public! Don't spend too much time talking to Him about your problems, because He already knows these things. I realized that when I talked about my difficulties and I noticed that every time I talked about my problems, they seemed to grow and become a mountain before me.

Continuously talking to God about our problems is not "praying" but "complaining". We are not really praying we are really only glorifying our problems before God.

Sometimes we say: *"Lord, you don't understand how bad this situation makes me feel,"* without knowing that God knows our circumstances quite well.

Perhaps God doesn't want you to speak about how big your issues are all the time. Perhaps He wants you to listen to what He has to say, so that you can realize how big He is in your life. God truly wants to share with you all the great things He has planned to do in your life and show you His power to fix all your problems.
Spending time with God from the early morning is the first step, a choice that will affect the whole day. Even if bad news comes, your reaction will be unique.

When you stay in prayer with the Lord, it creates a heavenly atmosphere around your life. When you go to His altar, anything that is not of God, burns away! I want to be a man of prayer and surround myself with people of prayer. People who pray affect your lifestyle and way of thinking, when they speak into your life, they speak with the guidance of the Holy Spirit.

Some people see a problem for every solution, and others have the solution to every problem! Those who pray have revelation, enlightenment and vision: when faced with a problem, they always see the way out.

When faced with an obstacle, Don't focus on it, but look for the way out! **While everyone sees the negative, you see an opportunity!**

A person who spends time with God brings light into the darkness, has hope when there is despair and knows the best thing to do in the most adverse circumstances. God guides them on the road they have to take. So, they aren't overwhelmed by the problems surrounding them; even better, they use them as a stepping stone. They give God's light, bring life and find a way. They can't help but have a good influence on others.

God is calling you to live in a new dimension. To do that, He sent the Holy Spirit to help, bless and transform you to become a blessing. He wants you to be a river of living water, not a lake of still water. He doesn't want us to be like marshy water as, with Him, we can be like rivers of fresh, clean waters flowing continuously to bring life to the desert. But everything starts on our knees!

Spending only a little bit of time with God is to stand with little effectiveness for Him. If we don't immerse ourselves in His presence, we lack effectiveness and can't transmit anything to others.

When we don't live in prayer, sometimes our words are so weak that they don't even get beyond the ceiling.

But when there is faithful prayer, our words become like sharp swords that breach into people's hearts. **In your mouth, God's words have the same power as in Jesus' mouth when He was on earth.** When you are full of Him, you'll see God speaking to others through you: as if you took the breath directly from His mouth and started giving His breath of life.

People who pray are people who, when they move, have heaven following them!

People who pray are people that don't tremble in the face of circumstances, but they themselves make circumstances tremble!

In your mouth, God's words have the same power as in Jesus' mouth when He was on earth!

Today I'm not going to pray that God blesses me, but I'm going to pray knowing that He has already blessed me!
When you pray, you are watering all the gifts God put into your heart; in His presence, the self you have created ceases to exist and all that is left is the true person He created!

NOTES

NOTES

DON'T SAY THAT YOU CAN'T DO
THE WILL OF GOD WHEN THERE IS
ABSOLUTELY NO SCRIPTURE THAT
AGREES WITH THAT! GOD SAYS:
YOU CAN DO IT!

- Francesco Basile

CHAPTER 4
DEEPER WITH GOD
PART II

There's nothing more crucial than having a life of prayer, a relationship with the Lord. Prayer isn't a religious act, as we are used to considering it, nor something you do by memory, like one does in a play. That is not prayer. When we repeat someone else's prayer, this indicates that we haven't understood the real heart at the base of prayer.

Prayer isn't a performance, but prayer is a relationship!
Prayer could be without words. It's similar to when a husband and wife reach a degree of knowledge and intimacy that they only need a look at each other to understand and perceive each other's thoughts. The same is true with the Lord: the more you spend time with Him, the more you can capture His heart, His glances, His impressions, and so much more.

> *Be ready in the morning, and then come up on Mount Sinai. Present yourself to me there on top of the mountain. No one is to come with you [...]*
> ***Exodus 34:2-3***

The second key I want to share is **WORSHIP**.

Why did God ask Moses to come up onto Mount Sinai? In the opening chapters of Exodus, Moses was shepherding his father-in-law's flock. He grew up in a royal palace, among prominent people of culture, learning good manners. But he was already hearing God's call upon his life.

His call for you is born within you, His call is already inside of you!

Jeremiah 1:5 states:

> *Before I formed you in the womb I knew you, before you were born I set you apart [...]*

God had already chosen you even before your parents thought to have you! Nobody is born by mistake, but we all came into existence by God's divine will! Maybe you weren't in your parents' plans, or they have told you that you were born by coincidence but, dear reader, I'm here to tell you that you aren't a mistake: you were born by God-incidence! How do you discover God's purpose for your life? Only by going up onto Mount Sinai. What is Sinai? It's the Mount on which Moses encountered God.

Moses felt called to set his people free. Hence one day, seeing an Egyptian beating a Hebrew, he intervened because he thought God was ready to use him. He acted on instinct by his strengths and killed the Egyptian man. However, that act was entirely fleshly and wrong. God couldn't use Moses without having an encounter with him first.

God had already chosen you even before your parents thought to have you!

If you haven't encountered God, even a good action will become a wrong one.
Moses took forty years in Pharaoh's palace to understand he wasn't as mighty and capable as he believed he was. Then he spent forty more years in the desert being a shepherd, and there he finally understood that God uses and wants to use people who are not self-important!

God often makes us walk around the long way, and we don't understand the reason. His plan will become clear only when you collide with Him, so that all that you have created, falls - and all that remains standing is what God has made! Moses had to shake off the identity he had built for himself, *"Pharaoh's grandson," "the great deliverer"* ... At Sinai, he understood that he could do nothing without God. God broke his pride.

You can experience God's grace only when your "self" breaks!

> *While they were worshiping the Lord and fasting, the Holy Spirit said, "Set apart for me Barnabas and Saul for the work to which I have called them."*
> **Acts 13:2**

They received the revelation of the Holy Spirit's plan during their prayer and worship.

When you fast, you're making room for the spiritual part of your life and feeding it.

Another version says: *"One day as they were worshiping God—they were also fasting as they waited for guidance."* For those who don't pray it's not easy to receive guidance from God.

Today so many things demand our time, energies, attention and health. So many things want to take your life away from you, but you have to let yourself be taken only by God! God's Spirit wants to bring you into His plans: God wanted you to be here at this very time and he has a plan for you. Please, don't live like everyone else.

"One day as they were worshiping [...]" I urge you to desire, look for, and do everything to find that day: that day in which you worship, you devote yourself to Him, you wait for guidance by fasting, prayer and worship.

Why fasting? Fasting doesn't make God move, but it makes you move towards God!

Fasting destroys your carnality and the authority of the body because *"man shall not live on bread alone, but on every word that comes from the mouth of God"*.

When you fast, you're making room for the spiritual part of your life and feeding it. When you devote lunch or dinner time to the Word and prayer, you're saying to your body: "God is my nourishment."

More than once, I happened to have minor health issues. After two or three days of fasting, my body responded by removing the pain.
Many people can't receive healing from God because their bodies have always commanded them and have supremacy over them: "smoke, eat!" Their bodies have always been in full charge.
If you let your body command you, you'll never be able to take authority over it when you need healing. If you let it be in charge for too long, it won't hear you. Therefore, get to working on taking back authority over your body.

Have you ever not wanted to go to church because your bed was warm and cozy? Or because the match was interesting, or a thousand other excuses? You need to overcome excuses because God has prepared so many blessings for you, and you have to go and take them in His presence.

***Fasting leaves aside your body
to get your spirit connected with heaven!***

When you get over the fleshly stimuli, you realize that the law of the Spirit is opposed to your carnality and that if you continue to obey your body, you could lose a great blessing!

Fasting is an act of intense worship! It leaves aside your body to get your spirit connected with heaven! In fasting, your spirit can get to the higher places, where God calls you to reign with Jesus Christ!
Fasting is the first thing I do when I feel that prayer isn't working! I fast when I don't feel like reading the Bible for days, because I

know it means that some area of my life is trying to drive me away from God! The flesh and sin will always keep you away from the Bible - but the Bible will always keep you away from those distractions.

A Bible falling apart represents someone who will never fall apart!

Worship is the only prayer language that takes you higher: it's not mind-made, nor made to inform God, but it's an act of worship!

> *Woman, I tell you that a new day is coming—in fact, it's already here—when it doesn't matter if we worship God here or in Jerusalem. The importance is not placed on the place of worship but on the way we worship. Is our worship spiritual and real? Do we have the help of the Holy Spirit? God is spirit, and his worshipers must have the guidance of His Spirit to worship Him the right way.*
> ### *John 4:21-23 [PARAPHRASE]*

That's why I add fasting to prayer. You may start by skipping a meal a week. I'm not telling you to begin with forty days of fasting, but I'm urging you to think about what you are doing. Is it bearing fruit? Is it arousing a new spiritual hunger within you? If so, then it is working, and you have discovered one of the keys to a higher level in God!

Not being hungry for the Word, nor God's presence is a clear symptom of spiritual illness: when you get sick, the first thing you lose is your appetite! On the other hand, being hungry is a sign of health. In such cases, we should put aside physical food to make room for the spiritual nourishment His Word gives us: that's what we truly need!

I have done some long fasts in my life. In those times, I received some amazing revelations I still treasure to this day. In those moments I felt God's presence so mightily in my life, that when I approached people, they immediately burst into tears or fell on their knees in prayer!

Every time Smith Wigglesworth, a man who witnessed all the miracles spoken of in the New Testament, got on a train, out-of-the-ordinary things began to happen. As he sat down in the wagon, everybody started crying, and then they approached him, asking what they needed to do to be saved. He had amazing results without even preaching!

The Bible says that while Peter was walking down the streets of Jerusalem, people hoped his shadow would fall on them that they might be healed! God's presence inside of him was so strong that Peter healed everything around him!

When you minister to the Lord, the Lord will minister to you!

In Acts 13, we read that the disciples were fasting, praying, and ministering to the Lord.

When you minister to the Lord, the Lord will minister to you! You'll see and feel His grace flowing onto your life. People around you will acknowledge that God is speaking through you. When you fast, pray, and worship, your voice and even your appearance will change!

I attended a conference in Sicily some time ago and I saw a woman walking with a cane. The doctors had told her that she wouldn't be able to walk naturally anymore. As I was preaching, God spoke to me, so I said to that woman: "Get up and walk, you can do it!" Then I helped her stand up from her seat and she started to run around the room, completely healed!

Some months after that incident, I was in Sicily in a restaurant, and I called the waitress to take my order. Guess who the waitress was? Yes, it was the woman healed during that conference. She had a job where she had to stand all day and walk back and forth - she was truly healed! When God works, he does things the perfect way! You can't worship God and stand in his presence only once a week. You must do this every day: you go up onto The Mountain like Moses every morning, because God wants to meet you there.

He longs to meet you more than you desire to meet Him. Just like a dad who can't wait for his child to come home safe and sound!

GOD'S FIRE MUST GET
INTO YOUR PLANS
*- **Francesco Basile***

CHAPTER 5
DEEPER WITH GOD
PART III

The first key we analyzed together is *get up, be ready in the morning.*

> *At each and every sunrise, I will give you every*
> *part of me; I will lay down on your altar any*
> *thought, hope, and dream of my heart. I will*
> *expose and submit every molecule of my life be-*
> *tween earth and heaven to your fire, waiting for*
> *your fire that only you can give me by your Spirit*
> *[...]*
> **Psalm 5:2-3 (TPT - paraphrase)**

You have to let God's fire sift through every thought, ambition, and desire of yours because, if God sends you, He also supports you! His fire must get into your plans. If it doesn't come from God, a project will lose strength, will cease to matter, so you will realize that He isn't behind it.

On the other hand, if a plan or a dream persists, you have to pray earnestly about it. Fast about it. If it keeps growing in your heart, then, my dear reader, it reasonably comes from God!

It is God who puts desires in your heart!

I can understand God's will when analyzing what is in my heart by investigating it through prayer and fasting. If it passes the test of the fire, then I will have directions about God's will!

Did you know that God's fire can visit your bodies? I don't know if you've ever felt a fire hitting you when you pray or when someone prays for you - a fire passing through you from head to toe. Whenever I feel it in my hands, I witness immediate healing in those for who I pray! The fire I'm talking about has to penetrate every molecule of your body - and that happens because you are submitting your body to God's power.

If this hasn't happened for a long time, the only way to turn up the heat again is by prayer, fasting, and revelation of the Word of God! When that happens, every single molecule of your body is submitting itself to God - and you feel it because you start walking, talking, and praying differently. When God's presence is alive, one can see the glory in the body!

In John 1:14, Scripture says that Jesus came to abide in a body of flesh. God's glory made its dwelling among humans! You can see God's glory only when the Word becomes flesh, not paper!

God's fire must get into your plans.

When His Word becomes your word, and His thoughts become your thoughts, all that you wish, ask for, and start dreaming is consistent with His Word. Jesus said: *ask and it will be given to you, you may ask me for anything according to my will, and I will give it to you!*

The second key we examined together is *WORSHIP, go up to the mountain.* To worship means to get carried away by the wind of the Spirit. To worship means to divest ourselves of all the things life puts on us - such as labels, stereotypes, patterns - to go back to being simple before God.

We saw that to worship means to minister to God. We often ask God to minister to us, but Scripture says that one receives in giving! As you learn to minister to God, you'll realize that He'll automatically minister to you! As you give yourself to Him, He will give Himself to you!

Sometimes, we have to do less to do more.

As Smith Wigglesworth said: *"Nothing of me but everything of God!"* When we pray, we shouldn't say: "Lord, give me more. I want more of you." We should say instead: "Lord, less of me" because God isn't holding Himself back from you; the problem is that you are too full of yourself!

Your "self" is reducing the room for God!

That's just like when your computer memory is full, and you have to unload it: when you are full of worries and things to do, it's vital to make room, removing what's unnecessary to make way to God. Sometimes it's the little things - and not the big problems or commitments - that rob you of what is significant.

Get rid of worries: leave them to God. Sometimes, we have to do less to do more.

The third key is *HAVE ACCESS, present yourself to me;*

> *Be ready in the morning, and then come up on Mount Sinai. Present yourself to me there on top of the mountain. No one is to come with you or be seen anywhere on the mountain; not even the*

flocks and herds may graze in front of the moun-
tain.

Exodus 34:2-3

In Scripture, God says to Moses: *"present yourself to me."* Have access! God is calling you to get close; He's inviting you to approach His presence. The desire to pray doesn't come from yourself. Bible says that God works in us to will and act: you pray because He calls you to do it (Philippians 2:13). You get up in the morning because God gives you the desire and strength to do it.

Sometimes, when I try to pray of my own will, I feel like I've been praying for three hours, even though it's only been three minutes. Why? Because there's a difference between when I pray of my own accord and when God, through His Spirit, calls me to do it! When your prayer stems from a fleshly desire, sense of duty, or obligation, it looks as if your words don't even get over the ceiling. On the other hand, sometimes you feel an urging attracting you. Scripture says: *"Draw me after you, let us run"* (Song of Songs 1:4). When you sense such an impulse, don't resist it!

The Holy Spirit knows the things we need and how to intercede for us through wordless groans! If you aren't getting answers, that means that you are praying on your own. The Holy Spirit wants to guide you. He knows how you have to pray. We ask for the things we wish, but God will not give us what we crave - because He wants to give us what we need!

With God, the significant thing is what He has to say - not what you have to say! Prayer mustn't convince God to be good because He already is: it must convince you that God is good!

Even youths grow tired and weary, and young
men stumble and fall; but those who hope in
the Lord will renew their strength. They will
soar on wings like eagles; they will run and not
grow weary, they will walk and not be faint.
Isaiah 40:30-31

We can translate the Hebrew *"hope"* as *"having a positive expectation on the Lord"* or as *"getting attached to God and completely depending on Him."* Those who have a positive expectation, who attach themselves to the Lord, who hope in Him, will renew their strength! Those are people who spend time before Him - and not people that, time after time, try to make God understand how serious their problems are. Those are the ones who stand before God saying: *"Lord, I'm here for you: I expect great things from you. I trust in you, and I'm leaning on you because I know that everything depends on you."*

We ask for the things we wish, but God will not give us what we crave - because He wants to give us what we need!

I found another rendering for the sentence *"renew their strength"*: *"[they will] trade their strength with God's."* There are things that you will never be able to do, but if you lean on the Lord, you'll do things that only Him can do by giving you His strength!
In my life, I did things I had neither the will nor the strength to do. When I got to know the Lord, I started to do the things of and from God! Just like Peter, when he walked upon the water. He didn't do just the things of God, but also the ones God asked him! Throughout the history of humankind until today, Jesus and Peter were the only ones able to walk upon the water.
Peter had a "positive expectation." Jesus spoke, and he obeyed, ready to attach to and depend on Him. He began to go down only

when he started to think about what he was doing. Jesus said to him: *"You of little faith!"* They often misinterpret that sentence. It doesn't mean that Peter had little faith because the Greek words are: "short-lived faith." Every time we rely on our strength instead of waiting for and hoping in the Lord, we stop walking in the supernatural.

It's easy to cast our weaknesses on God because we don't want them; the hard part is to leave Him our strength, pride, reputation, talents, and all we have built for ourselves.

Sometimes the worst enemy of the best things is the good things.

We often can't wait for God to take our problems! But God is asking us for the things we like! Those who trade their strength with God's will soar into the air! Maybe someone told you that you couldn't walk and some other that you will not be able to run, but God is saying that you can fly!

Don't worry if you feel that they've broken your legs so that you can't walk because God is giving you a pair of wings to fly high!

"They will soar on wings like eagles, up to the sky. They will get airborne and reach the top!"

Studying the life of the eagles, I found that they are wondrous creatures! They don't fly with their strength but look for a high place like a tree or a mountain. There they wait for the most suitable wind and then go with it by spreading their enormous wings! They might seem small and insignificant, but they're majestic when opening their wings. If you see yourself as small and unimportant, it means you haven't understood that God isn't calling you to live like a chicken pecking on the ground: He is calling you to lift high like an eagle!

***Maybe someone told you that you couldn't walk and
some other that you will not be able to run,
but God is saying that you can fly!***

Another characteristic of eagles is the ability to recognize winds! Scripture says that the Holy Spirit is like a wind that wants to blow under your wings. You should be like an eagle, learning to recognize His voice and the proper time. When the time comes, my friends, don't worry if you can't run because you weren't born to run - you were born to fly! It won't be your strength nor capabilities that will take you up - it will be those of God!

> *Therefore, I urge you, brothers and sisters, in view of God's mercy, to offer your bodies as a living sacrifice, holy and pleasing to God—this is your true and proper worship. Do not conform to the pattern of this world, but be transformed by the renewing of your mind [...]*
> **Romans 12:1-2**

God made the first move towards you, a move called Jesus! Now He's waiting for us to take a step towards Him. His move to you is called grace, and your move towards Him is called faith!

We all are living sacrifices. At the Old Testament times, the offerings were dead. They were placed before the altar and remained there to burn for God. We as sacrifices should put our lives on the altar and stay there, but some of us often roll away from it. We are a living sacrifice; therefore, God expects that we offer ourselves on the altar to serve Him, give Him our lives, and make a difference.

GOD'S GLORY MANIFESTING ITSELF
IN PUBLIC IS, AND WILL ALWAYS BE,
THE RESULT OF A RELATIONSHIP
WITH THE FATHER IN PRIVATE
- Francesco Basile

CHAPTER 6
DEEPER WITH GOD
PART IV

The fourth key is *WITHDRAW* - no one is to come with you.

> *Yet the news about him spread all the more, so that crowds of people came to hear him and to be healed of their sicknesses. But Jesus often withdrew to lonely places and prayed.*
> **Luke 5:15-16**

In the middle of a revival, as everybody was asking Him questions, Jesus knew that the key to that revival wasn't people, but the Father! If I had been in the middle of a revival, I wouldn't have chosen to withdraw to lonely places. I would have remained there to see healings and freed people gathering to hear the messages. I would have stayed there. Nonetheless, everything concerning God is different: if you want to go up, you have to learn to go down! With God, the roads to high places go through the low places! As the crowd was looking for Him, Jesus was fighting to defend His time alone with His Dad.

God's glory manifesting itself in public is, and will always be, the result of a relationship with the Father in private!
You can withdraw with God because Jesus died to provide the anointing, but you have to die to yourself to protect it! Many are no longer seeing God's anointing in their lives, no longer feeling the

fire of the Holy Spirit, nor having revelations, nor seeing results, because they got caught up with busyness rather than the anointing, the wind, and God's Spirit.

Every morning, after telling the Lord what I have to say to Him, I remain silent and wait for Him. At that moment, plenty of thoughts, concerns, and things that need to be done come to my mind. These thoughts crowding your mind when you start to pray, were actually there all along, all you have to do is to acknowledge them and then leave them at the Lord's feet.

"Be still, and know that I am God."

Don't give up while you're in prayer, don't fight with your mind nor with your strength! Just learn to stay there, telling the Lord from the inside: I'm here for you! I worship you!

Suddenly you'll feel something changing. Those thoughts disappear, giving way to God's presence.
I'm here to tell you that you've been content for too long with staying in His courts or in the Holy Place, where your thoughts, in the end, won. Go further! There's so much more for you in the Most Holy place! There you'll feel another atmosphere and hear another voice telling you: "There's more for you!"

> ***Prayer is not only to do with speaking,***
> ***but rather having intimacy with God.***

In contrast to what you have probably learned, dear readers, there's one thing you have to know about prayer: it is **intimacy**. It's not a monologue, but a dialogue: it's a communication with God. In prayer, you get to know Him better and in the meantime, you know yourself and the plan God has for you. God amazingly uses your silence in prayer to talk to you and show you who you are in Him!

IF YOU WANT TO SEE RESULTS
HERE ON THE EARTH, YOU HAVE
TO SEE THEM IN HEAVEN FIRST!

- Francesco Basile

CHAPTER 7
YOU CAN FIND YOURSELF
IN GOD'S PRESENCE

Whenever I get close to God, He tells me who I am; my real identity in Him emerges!

I immediately notice if I'm praying with my mind or with my spirit. If you ever have spoken empty and repeated words, know that that's not spontaneous communication but a religious ritual! On the other hand, sometimes you realize that there are moments when you feel the power of fellowship and intimacy even if you keep silent. I want you to know that communication in prayer isn't always a verbal one: **prayer goes from heart to heart - not from mouth to ear!**

Prayer is understanding one another: like a husband and wife understand each other with a single glance, you do the same with God in prayer. There you become aware that God is more real than the floor under your feet! In His presence, we see all the lies and fortresses we built falling. I may tell someone: "I love you," but my heart is far from them. However, God's word says: *"That person should not expect to receive anything from the Lord. Such a person is double-minded [...]"*

When you are before God and discover true prayer, then you'll find the real you!

People often build walls so thick around them that they can't be free even in prayer to be themselves.

When we pray, we have to abandon every insecurity and create real intimacy, so that all we have built through the years - and that doesn't come from God - can fall! Before God, you can't pretend to be someone else: you have to take off all the lies and masks the world has stuck to you and clothe yourself with the truth He has for you. But unless you learn to do it before God, you won't be able to do it before people!

Before God, you can't pretend to be someone else: you have to take off all the lies and masks the world has stuck to you and clothe yourself with the truth He has for you. But unless you learn to do it before God, you won't be able to do it before people!

With God, even the thickest of masks can dissolve. He knows where your wrinkles and flaws are: you may make fun of anyone, even yourself, but not God.

When we let the masks fall, allowing the Holy Spirit to bring forth the good that He deposited a long time ago in our hearts and that He sees in us, the disguises fall, the glance changes. There's a new light on our faces: not because those who pray are somehow special, but because they are free from everything that takes them away from God.

A person who can stand in life is someone who has learned how to be on their knees.

The great preacher Charles H. Spurgeon once said: *"One single faithful person with God can form the greatest majority in the universe."*

What you receive, become, discover about yourself, and God reveals to you in prayer, gives you the certainty that you're doing exactly what He showed you **right there in prayer**. When we have such an intimacy with God, there's a "download" from heaven to our hearts, and God shows us who we are in His presence and what we can do in life.

> *The next day John was there again with two of his disciples. When he saw Jesus passing by, he said, "Look, the Lamb of God!"*
> **John 1:35-37**

John could not have said this, if he wasn't sure. He had that certainty because what he had seen in natural reality, was exactly what God had shown him in his vision!

> *Then John gave this testimony: "I saw the Spirit come down from heaven as a dove and remain on him. [...]"*
> **John 1:32**

As already said, Smith Wigglesworth was a marvelous minister of God! The Holy Spirit used to talk very clearly to him: before he went out, the Spirit used to show him unbelievable details about what Wigglesworth would have done on that day, where he would have gone, and how he would have worked. Sometimes he received in prayer the exact address of the houses to go to, the sort of illness or difficulty troubling one or more people in those houses, and what to do about them. How did he do this? He learned to see in the invisible! He used to see details, receive instruction, obtain "downloads from heaven," and then change the earth.

If you want to see results here on the earth,
you have to see them in heaven first!

A person without prayer is a limited one who can only see through their physical eyes. A person who prays has the eyes of the heart enlightened.

Prayer unlocks your life, giving you the key to becoming what God meant you to be in Him. Prayer is not a routine. Many people think it's boring thing because they never really tasted the real depth of God's presence.

***If you want to see results here on the earth, you have to
see them in heaven first!***

Scripture says that sometimes Jesus spent the whole night praying. I want to encourage you to start praying at night or in the early morning because those are the only moments when you are free from any other voice. We are more predisposed to listen to God's voice; there are no distractions; all is calm; our minds slow down. In the daytime, however, the mind moves too fast because thousands of thoughts bomb it!

> *As David said in the Scriptures:*
> *"At midnight I rise to give you thanks [...]"*
> ***Psalm 119:62***

God doesn't want you to pray only for your needs; instead, He desires that you pray because you want to take care of the things on His heart.

Don't pray that God bless your projects,
but pray that He will use you for His.

The time has come when God doesn't just bless your life, for the Lord wants to make you a blessing to others! People need to see not only a blessed man or woman, but a man or a woman able to bless those around them too. When people look at you, they must see Jesus!

Maybe you grew up with the idea that one must sit forever in a place of worship, but Jesus hasn't saved you to see you sitting on a chair nor stuck silently in a church. He saved you because He wants you to become a flame of fire for His reign! He wants you to be a flame for Him! When asked: *"How do you draw hundreds of thousands of people to your evangelistic meetings?"* Reinhard Bonnke, one of the greatest evangelists of our century, answered: *"I found that in the presence of God I catch fire - and people always come to see a man on fire that doesn't burn up!"*

Prayer releases cloves of heaven that you can take with you!

During one of my visits to Sicily, I preached about the cross. I said that when we think about the cross, we usually imagine it with Jesus hanging on it. But Jesus went to the cross in our place - in everybody's place:

> *[…] one died for all […]*
> ***2 Corinthians 5:14***

Therefore, on the cross, we are there together with Jesus: just as in a group portrait. And similarly, as you would look for yourself in group photographs, you have to do the same with the cross! While I was speaking on that, the Lord spoke to me about a girl in the audience. So, I summoned her and prayed and prophesied over her. As soon as I started to pray, she burst into tears: something supernatural was happening in her life. After the meeting, I asked her why she had cried. She replied that she had dreamed of me - although she didn't know me yet and hadn't ever seen me before - I told her in the dream to come and take a group picture with the church youth group. But she didn't feel worthy of being part of that group, so she revealed to me the sentence: **"The cross is like a group photograph, and you have to look for yourself in it..."** had deeply been impressed on her heart. That girl still serves God today and has seen great miracles in her life, marriage and work. God had told that girl in Sicily about me, what I would be preaching on, and the importance of identifying oneself with the cross of Christ. I'd say that this is being in the right place at the right time with the right people! God communicates with us, wondrously guiding us!

He saved you because He wants you to become a flame of fire for His reign!

I could report hundreds of experiences like that. Once, I was preaching in France, and God told me that there was a man in the room whose family members had been snatched away on account of of the Gospel in a persecuted nation. At that moment, a loud cry of pain and liberation came out from this man. He was a former Muslim, a refugee, whose wife and son had been murdered after his conversion to Christianity: he himself had been tortured in the desert and left there to die. But he had survived and managed to escape from his land. That word in that day changed his life, giving him the certainty that God was with him and his loved ones. God gave him a precise word that freed him from all his pain, forever!

To serve the Lord means to report on earth what you've heard in heaven!

It's crucial to realize that serving God doesn't want to preach only on Sundays, singing a few songs during worship, or only telling people that God loves them. It means to listen, hear from God and report on earth what you've heard in heaven! To carry heaven with you wherever you go! God is looking for this type of people! You must be intentional and enter God's business being hungry for more of Him. It is his pleasure to give this type of person everything they need to fulfill their destiny in Him!

IT'S ONLY THERE THAT YOU
CAN FIND THAT SWEET POWER
WORKING PROFOUNDLY
IN YOUR HEART
- Francesco Basile

Chapter 8
PRAYER OPENS
YOUR EYES

True prayer makes us enter into revelation, opening our eyes to see the spiritual realms, invisible to the human eye. It allows us to go beyond, letting us see with God's eyes His higher reality. The things we look at are temporary and subject to change, but the things of God are everlasting, unchangeable. That makes us understand that the things we can't see are more durable than visible ones! When you can see the invisible, you can do the impossible.

Prayer is a way of life, and we don't have to beg God to make Him listen to us. Jesus already did everything for us! Because of the sacrifice and resurrection of Christ, we can have a continuous communion with Him. If we have an attitude of intimacy and worship, we can live a life of prayer 24/7!

Prayer is to be aware of God despite the circumstances, the place where you are and the voices filling your head.
It's clear that there are different depths of prayer. It's often the Holy Spirit Who draws you to withdraw in lonely places - just like He did with Jesus. Being alone with God is a priority for those that choose to be God's servants. We don't have to be afraid of being lonely, because some answers will not come unless we live some moments with Him alone. The majority of people view loneliness as a bad thing, but it's not always true. It becomes such when taken

to the extreme, but if you withdraw with God for some time, it will be a blessing; your room will become a slice of heaven!

Do not escape loneliness: sometimes it's a need. Sometimes you may wake up in the middle of the night. If so, bow down on your knees and ask God if it's Him Who wants you to be awake to listen to His voice. On some occasions, the only moment when God can talk to us is the night time because, in the daytime, we have so many things to think about that we can't listen to what He has to say. In such cases, keep a notebook next to you to write down all the words the Holy Spirit reveals to you. The Lord wants to make sure you live unique experiences that go beyond the ordinary prayer. He wants to bring you to places where you will hear the angels singing and see indescribable things. You don't have to be afraid of living supernatural experiences; on the contrary, we have to look increasingly for and expect more of them. God wants to make us to have and live out experiences we will carry for the rest of our lives!

If you want to see things others have never seen, you have to do what others have never done!
Why did Jesus remain forty days in the wilderness? Because the Holy Spirit guided Him there and stayed with Him even when the devil tempted Him.

You're probably wondering: "How can I overcome temptations?" Dear reader, you can do it only when the Holy Spirit gives you the right words. During those forty days, Jesus was indeed tempted, but it's also true that He made His relationship with the Holy Spirit grow! **Extreme loneliness brought Him to extreme power!**

Do you want to see more in your life? You need more intimacy! It's only there that you can find that sweet power working profoundly in your heart!

Years ago, one of my Bible school students told me: "In the past, I tried to 'obtain' God's presence, to get the skies open, so that God would hear me. But now, thank God, I have realized that the skies are already open thanks to Jesus Christ's resurrection. Now I know that He wants to communicate with me at every moment of the day!"

> *And so, dear brothers, now we may walk right into the very Holy of Holies, where God is, because of the blood of Jesus. This is the fresh, new, life-giving way that Christ has opened up for us by tearing the curtain—his human body— to let us into the holy presence of God.*
> **Hebrews 10:19-20 (TLB)**

Prayer reveals to me who I am and who God is. I find God in it, but I also find the authentic me without masks or filters.

Prayer changes your perspective on your way of being, personality, and way of facing certain circumstances. Consequently, you learn to see the daunting situations as strong points from which you can start again. In prayer, you rise high and see the circumstances as God sees them: it's Him Who gives us His perspective. When you look at things from a human viewpoint, you almost always will stumble onto something wicked because limiting God is a diabolic thing.

When you pray, God brings down the lies you've always believed in.

If we don't approach His presence, we will always keep carrying around all the lies with which we have used. It's only in His presence that we leave everything before His throne, getting rid of it forever. Prayer makes you authentic again.

I could spend months speaking about the things Jesus told me and tells me every day - and that might encourage you a little - but listening to what He has to say to you only for five minutes changes all!

In prayer, seek to find the perspective of God, see yourself as He sees you. When you spend time in His presence, the earthly things no longer matter, and you start value what God values.

Through prayer, you revive your spiritual sensitivity for the day ahead, not only for that moment. God has many things to tell you every day, but he will not necessarily speak to you when you are in His presence. He could do so at other moments through wither an image, a person, or a situation. God is limitless.

We have to recognize every good thing in and around us in Christ. Let me give you an example: let's say you're driving and a thought comes to you: "Today God hasn't spoken to me... my prayer was useless." Then you instinctively feel to turn right, so you do and you don't even know that if you had gone straight, you would have had an accident that would have ruined your life.

Our spirits love to pray, but our carnality, occupied with many other things, doesn't want to pray. Dear reader, know that we need to "sacrifice the human part" to make way for the spiritual things, the things that truly matter. You will be able to rule your life and have command and victory over any circumstance by submitting your fleshly needs to your spiritual needs.

In prayer, you will find the things God has prepared for you, the road He has traced for you, and the dominion over all life's situations. When you pray, your influence as kings and queens on this earth increases.

> *[...] made us alive with Christ even when we were dead in transgressions—it is by grace you have been saved. And God raised us up with Christ and seated us with him in the heavenly realms in Christ Jesus [...]*
> **Ephesians 2:5-6**

We don't pray as victims of the circumstances, but rather from a position far above the circumstances. We are at God's right hand in Christ, seated in the heavenly realms.

Don't pray about your problems, but pray about God's solutions. One thing is saying: "Lord, you know my problems; you know how much I'm hurting." One other is saying: "Thank you, Father, that you always answer me. Thank you that you make me see things from another viewpoint - and the situation I'm facing is nothing compared to what Jesus faced!"

It's quite clear that praying about solutions differs from praying about problems. It's not about what we have to say to God, but it's about what He has to tell us. We often don't realize that what He is saying to us is the solution to what we're about to ask Him! As soon as we focus on His things, He automatically takes care of our needs!

FASTING ISN'T SOMETHING
WE DO EVERY ONCE IN A WHILE;
IT SHOULD BE PART OF OUR
LIFESTYLES

- Francesco Basile

CHAPTER 9

PRAYER CHANGES EVERYTHING

Every time God makes something great throughout history it takes place through someone. We can see that these great steps of action were always characterized by a time of prayer. When Moses got up to the mountain, he fasted for forty days. And right about then he received the Ten Commandments. Scripture says God Himself wrote the Law on the tablets with His finger in front of Moses. Whenever Moses spent time in God's presence, his face used to shine. It was as if God's glory shined through his face. That suggests that fasting and prayer causes our bodies to mirror God's glory.

Fasting allows you to go deeper. Nothing else does, only intensified prayer! If you have fasted before, you may have noticed its benefits from the first few hours.

Fasting and prayer earnestly calls us to get serious with God. You immediately sense and experience something happening; you feel that you're experiencing something great. This inspires you to go even deeper. For instance: I have often wanted to start a prolonged fast again, although not knowing how many days it will last. As soon as I start fasting, I realize how much my relationship with the Lord had weakened. As I gradually regain spiritual strength, all the revelations God had given me in the last season, come to mind again.

The truth is that when you fast, it's as if a new world is opening up. It's a commitment to God: you feel open and prepared to receive something more intense. You realize you don't want to keep living only with what you already have, but you desire something else; you want more and never feel satisfied. **Fasting is a position within yourself, in which you say: I'm not satisfied, there's more for me; there's more in my body, more of me that has to give glory to God.**

When I fast and pray, my body is a clearer channel, more sensitive to the flow of God's presence and Spirit. Nonetheless, you can't realize it until you fast and see the difference! Instead of thinking about eating and resting, you think: "I have to read, meditate, write..."

Fasting keeps you awake, responsive. Ready to dedicate your time to the Lord, in fasting you regain time in the spirit. That alone would be worth it. Instead of sitting for two hours eating, you spend two hours praying!
We have allowed our bodies to command us for too long when we, as children of God, should be led by Him. Sensations, pains, feelings, cravings, weariness mustn't drive us, for they mustn't be the ruling factors! When having an issue, many people immediately try to understand how to solve it by buying books and resources on the subject. The same is true with those who always eat sweets, without ever brushing their teeth, and then they have to run to the dentist.

The truth is that when you fast, it's as if a new world is opening up. It's a commitment to God: you feel open and prepared to receive something more intense. You realize you don't want to keep living only with what you already have, but you want more; you want more of God and won't be content without it.

Many times, at the beginning of my faith experience, I didn't feel like going to church on Sunday: every inch of me wanted to stay home. I remember when that happened, I used to take a stand against the "I don't feel like it," and would decide to go. Once there, God talked to me and blessed me through the sermon!

We must walk with God.

When I'm praying, I love to say to the Lord: *"Father, may your presence permeate every organ of my body. May you invade every part of my body. May every cell of my body let your glory shine!"*

Fasting isn't something we do every once in a while; it should be part of our lifestyles

Don't wait for something to happen before training your body to react to God's presence. Start disciplining it now! Paul says: *"I strike a blow to my body and make it my slave"* (1 Corinthians 9:27). Your body is a tool that must serve God's original intent, His purpose. You mustn't serve it, but you must take care of it. Fasting is food education. It's not something we do every once in a while; it should be something which is part of our lifestyles. You have to keep working to submit your body because you can't do it in one day. The same is true with the mind: you have to renew it daily.

If I begin to overlook fasting, I immediately feel that I'm eating more and overdoing it. Here's the difference: when you fast, you're controlling your body, and when you overeat, you realize you are submitting to your body. It's a mere exaggerated carnal desire.

73

I have the right to do anything, but I will not be mastered by anything.

I remember that, some time ago, I read about Reverend Kenneth Hagin, who loved to drink Coke, especially in summer. He used to drink one after another, until one day he realized that he had become addicted to it. Only then he understood that this issue was dominating him, so he decided never to drink it again in his entire life. And it was indeed so.

Discipline and constancy, characterize the men and women of God we look up to. The Bible says: *"The man of God is not given to drunkenness. Who's given to drunkenness? The one who is addicted!"*

Fasting puts you back in line; therefore, it's essential to fast frequently, even once or twice a week, and not once a year or a month.

> *I have not departed from the commands of his lips; I have treasured the words of his mouth more than my daily bread.*
> **Job 23:12**

The Word of God must be for you more important than physical food. Think about it. What is more important than food? Like oxygen and water, food is essential for life. We are so used to having food on our tables and drinkable water accessible anywhere, that we don't realize that those are products without which we would die. In the above verse, Job states that it was more important for him to eat spiritual food than natural: the significance of God's Word exceeded that of his life.

You can depend on the Word of God, and your body must know about it. Your life doesn't depend on food but on the nourishment that comes from heaven. Satan tempted Jesus by saying: *"tell this stone to become bread."* But Jesus answered: *"Man shall not live by bread alone, but by every word of God."*

The Word coming from God must be like nourishment for you; don't think of it as a book to read, neither as an idol. The Bible won't do your life any good if it stays closed. It will make an true difference only when it becomes life and bread for you. You have to start chewing and digesting it so that it can kick in.

When I ask people what God told them in the last 24 hours, people often have wide eyes, as if to say: "I don't even know if He ever talked to me!" What kind of relationship do you have with the Word of the Lord? Is it only a book to you? You should hear God speaking and listen to Him daily. No day should pass without you having an impression, a vision, an image, a sensation, or a sentence from God.

I want and desire that you have an authentic relationship with the Lord: not with a book, but with its Author. The Bible is the only book whose Author is near you as you read, explaining it step by step.

Your life doesn't depend on food but on the nourishment that comes from heaven.

A believer who believes is a danger to hell!

We are the ones limiting God's power because He is limitless. Your body tries to limit you but when you pray and fast, every cell in your body starts to obey. Jesus wants to manifest Himself through your body, voice, eyes, to the point that even your cells will exude His anointing.

T.L. Osborn used to talk about his crusades, and there were always sorcerers, wizards, and Muslims ready to kill him. Nevertheless, he used to stand in front of thirty, forty, sometimes more than one hundred thousand people, sure that something grand would take place once again! Osborn shares how he called on stage all the lepers in a hall, and thirteen people went up. After this, he also invited on stage all the Muslim leaders, asking them to pray for those lepers, but nothing happened. T.L. Osborn wanted to show people Jesus; therefore, he touched the first leper, and leprosy disappeared. The same happened with the other lepers so that all 13 lepers were instantly healed. On that day, all the Muslims converted and gave their lives to Jesus.

> **A person of prayer never utters their own words;**
> **a person of prayer has heavenly words**
> **coming naturally from their mouth.**

That's the dimension God wants for us, but how can we get it? By bending our lives, carnality, projects, and all that tries to restrain and drive us away from God. The devil will always try to limit your conscience by saying that you are not worth it, but he will never be able to touch your life, your anointing because it comes from God. When you fast and pray, people feel that. A person of prayer never utters their own words; a person of prayer has heavenly words coming naturally from their mouth. Often without knowing it, we are limiting God's work in us. It's not God, but it's us. Fasting makes you realize that.

Whenever you realize that you don't want to spend time with the Lord or whenever you don't feel like reading or praying, start fasting! There's no fasting better than another, but the important thing is that you start with a few hours - then the more you become familiar, the more you will see the benefits. The key is staying hydrated because water is good for the body in many ways and frees it from the toxins in the food we've eaten.

I always recommend beginning with skipping one meal a day, then gradually taking this to 24 hours without food. After gaining more and more confidence, under Holy Spirit's guidance and possibly in a state of excellent health, try and then fast over 36 hours. But it also depends on the sort of day or week you're going to face. Always use wisdom! In my opinion, the three-days fast, in which I usually drink a lot of water and sometimes infusions, is really useful. When I go this length of fasting, I can sense the difference; even hunger is not as hard as in the first few days. It's like my body has already lost the supremacy it had on me. God's Spirit communicates with me, and His voice seems so clear; I easily understand Scripture and get a new perspective in the Word. Nevertheless, that's a training that needs time and practice. Start with small steps, and be sure to drink a lot of water (two liters a day), also try and put lemon juice in your water.

Add to your creed an action.

We need to start experiencing God to understand Him more and see more of Him. If you believe it, do something!

Believers use to believe and act! If you want to do something great for Jesus, do it and do it big - and even if you make a mistake, do it big, as long as you decide to do it! We can't even imagine how many people are in the valley of indecision, never doing anything but just keep waiting for the perfect moment. But God is with those who move and those who act!

Peter was the only man throughout history who was able to walk on water with Jesus: Scripture says that Jesus caught his hand as Peter was sinking, then they got back in the boat with Jesus. At first, Peter walked alone, and then he did it with Jesus. He ventured out is the key here: if he waited for everyone else to give him consent, he would never got down out of the boat.

Ifs and buts steal your greatest blessings.
Fasting is to submit ourselves: I decide to be a spiritual man, I choose to be more than what I am; I want to enter what God has called me to do and be; I'm not going to settle for anything less.

The Gospel doesn't consist of words; the Gospel is power.
Today more than ever, many people try to persuade you, brainwash you, and make you reflect, reason, rationalize the things of God. On the other hand, God says that your faith must be power-based, and not wisdom-based! People don't need wisdom but need might! And God wants to give that might to you today.

> *People don't need wisdom but need might! And God wants to give that might to you today.*

Even though there are natural times and seasons to do certain activities, God can make you go beyond time. Your faith in Him can accelerate time.

In the name of Jesus, you can get in fifteen days what others get in fifteen years. God is limitless. We have acquired this world's system, but God isn't tied to the mental limits surrounding us. Even though He intervenes over time, He isn't temporal because He is everlasting. Though we are temporary beings, God looks at us from an everlasting perspective. God called Abram "father of a multitude" when he wasn't even Isaac's father yet. Why? Because God was already seeing him in eternity!

In Psalm 139, David says: *"My frame was not hidden from you."* God sees you in and from eternity. He has already seen the day of your birth and your end. When you pray and fast you connect with God, you are taking something that would have happened to you in the future and bringing it here today by faith. There's no future nor past for God, but only today, the present - He is the everlasting present.

Take something in God's space and bring it into yours.

WHEN STUDYING THE WORD, WE ADD WOOD TO THE FIRE. WHEN FASTING, WE COMPACT THE WOOD AND REVIVE THE FLAME.

- Francesco Basile

Chapter 10

TEN BENEFITS OF FASTING

1. Fasting reactivates our spiritual senses.

> *Declare a holy fast; call a sacred assembly. Summon the elders and all who live in the land to the house of the Lord your God, and cry out to the Lord.*
> ***Joel 1:14***

We fast so that God's fire, the passion for His work, and the progress of His reign might burn again in His Church's heart.

We fast because we believe that even though God is ready to pour the abundance of His grace on us, He waits for our firm and concrete invitation.

Fasting keeps us on guard, attentive, with our spiritual eyes wide open, and ready for the next step the Holy Spirit asks us to take. Through fasting, we as a church take possession of the might and the blessings God has planned for us for a long time.

2. Fasting teaches us how to worship.

Woman, I tell you that a new day is coming—in fact, it's already here—when it doesn't matter if we worship God here or in Jerusalem. The importance is not placed on the place of worship but on the way we worship. Is our worship spiritual and real? Do we have the help of the Holy Spirit? God is spirit, and his worshipers must have the guidance of His Spirit to worship Him the right way.

John 4:21-23 [PARAPHRASE]

True worship is not just for a moment, but it's a lifestyle. It's a life spent in search of the plan God has for us and devoted to accomplishing His work - not for a day nor for an era. Worship is dedicating our lives to God right now.

The Holy Spirit wishes to guide and teach us what to do and with whom to be. We often try to give God what we consider appropriate, but only the Holy Spirit can give us the keys to walk as God asks us to walk. He alone can reveal to us the purpose to which He has prepared for us before time.

True worship is not just for a moment, but it's a lifestyle.

3. Fasting clears the road.

[...] Jehoshaphat resolved to inquire of the Lord, and he proclaimed a fast for all Judah.

2 Chronicles 20:3

When we have a project or a dream in our hearts, one way to discern if what we think is actually from God and that is by fasting and prayer. Fasting is the secret key to unlock the treasures of heaven and remove everything that doesn't come from God!

It's not a diet, but refraining from food for a spiritual purpose.

Fasting causes a higher sensitivity towards the things of God, fasting clears our minds from the thoughts that continuously crowd our minds and weigh us down.

Some spiritual areas activate and develop only through prayer and fasting.

If Jesus could have carried out His ministry without prayer and fasting, He would not have needed to withdraw for forty days in the wilderness to fast. Above all, why did the Spirit lead Him in that direction? The simple answer is: some spiritual areas activate and develop only through prayer and fasting.

Put your projects on the altar today, and then, through prayer and fasting, let God guide you to the best He has for you.

4. Fasting makes us enter the great things of God.

> *Very truly I tell you, whoever believes in me will do the works I have been doing, and they will do even greater things than these, because I am going to the Father.*
> **John 14:12**

During His ministry on earth, Jesus showed that He could move in the supernatural power of God through fasting and prayer. His authority over demons was the result of His connection with the Father through the Holy Spirit. Jesus Himself tells us: you can do it too! If we want to have the outcomes Jesus had and that of His disciples, we must have a spiritual lifestyle focused on fasting and prayer.

5. Fasting awakens our lives.

> *Is not this the kind of fasting I have chosen: to loose the chains of injustice and untie the cords of the yoke, to set the oppressed free and break every yoke?*
> **Isaiah 58:6**

Prayer and fasting awaken our awareness about who we are in Christ. Our bodies are God's temple: He chose to pour in and through us His power. We have to consecrate ourselves through prayer and fasting. God's kingdom consists of power. God loves to pour His might out on us to set the oppressed free and heal our cities.

Choose to become a mighty tool in His hands today!

6. Fasting is a form of consecration to God.

> *Therefore, I urge you, brothers and sisters, in view of God's mercy, to offer your bodies as a living sacrifice, holy and pleasing to God—this is your true and proper worship.*
> **Romans 12:1**

Consecrate your life to God again during your time of prayer and fasting. You'll find a great connection with God, and you'll experience His love more intensely.

In your time of prayer and fasting, ask God for clarification about:

- His vision for your life
- the job He has for you
- the areas in your life where you need God's help to change and grow

7. Fasting puts our lives on God's altar.

> *Return to me with all your heart, with fasting*
> *[...]*
> **Joel 2:12**

Fasting breaks the power of routine. It's a form of worshiping God that renews our bodies, souls, and spirits, restoring order and divine priority in our lives. Scripture urges us *"to offer your bodies as a living sacrifice, holy and pleasing to God"* (Romans 12:1).

Fasting brings us back on our knees, reminds us how much we need God and His grace, and inspires us to seek greater depth with God.

Fire always falls on a sacrifice well placed on the spiritual altar of prayer and fasting. Let us prepare today so that this glorious fire falls on us.

8. Fasting prepares us for supernatural experiences.

In most cases, any great spiritual experience you and I, or any person in Scripture, has had and will have, is the outcome of a time of prayer.

9. Fasting opens us to divine guidance.

While they were worshiping the Lord and fasting, the Holy Spirit said, "Set apart for me Barnabas and Saul for the work to which I have called them."
Acts 13:2

Worship is not merely singing: it also involves our commitment in fasting.

Our fasting never goes unnoticed by the Holy Spirit. In most cases, the Holy Spirit Himself awakens the desire for fasting in our hearts, intending to communicate something to us. In the above Scripture passage, prophets and teachers in the Antioch church were assembled and were fasting. Then the Holy Spirit prophetically said to them: *"Set apart for me Barnabas and Saul for the work to which I have called them."* God even today calls men and women to carry out works, but first of all, His call requires preparation and commitment through prayer, meetings and Word reading. Let us pray today that the same Lord who noticed Paul and Barnabas' worship may accept ours, and use us to make His kingdom progress.

When studying the Word, we add wood to the fire. When fasting, we compact the wood and revive the flame

10. Fasting helps us refocus our faith.

If you find it hard to focus on God things in reading, in prayer, in your time with the Lord, then you need to rekindle the fire within you. When studying the Word, we add wood to the fire. When fasting, we compact the wood and revive the flame. Fasting removes the strength of everything getting in the way of your time and connection with God. The enemy would like to break the pace of your relationship with the Lord by trying to distract you from what matters. So, make sure to reinvigorate God's flame through prayer and fasting.

FASTING ACTS AS A CATALYST FOR
GOD'S ACTIVITIES AND AS
A FIRE-EXTINGUISHER FOR
THE FLESHLY ACTIVITIES.
- Francesco Basile

Chapter 11

A HOLY LACK
OF SATISFACTION

*Trust [rely on and have confidence] in the Lord
and do good. Dwell in the land and feed [secure-
ly] on His faithfulness. Delight yourself in the
Lord, and He will give you the desires and peti-
tions of your heart.*
Psalm 37:3-4 (AMP)

God indeed puts dreams and projects in our hearts, but also a holy
lack of satisfaction, as a sign that there is something expired, out-
dated and without vitality.

God gave you an inner holy discontent or frustration as an indicator for an old and stagnant era, to point out that there is something
new waiting for you.

The holy lack of satisfaction coming from the Holy Spirit usually
requires significant changes in our lifestyles, attitudes, settings, and
prayer styles that are now static and unfruitful. What do we do
when we have such a spiritual deposit in our hearts?

1. KNOWING

**Knowing if it comes from God through prayer and
fasting.**

- Fasting acts as a catalyst for more of God's activities and as a fire-extinguisher for the fleshly activities. Many people don't realize how much they are in the flesh - sometimes even for years. We often are so convinced of a view that not even God can make us think otherwise.
- A prolonged fasting time becomes like a light in the dark of our hearts that illuminates us and points out things we didn't notice before.
- Fasting annihilates all the fleshly convictions that have a spiritual shape but no spiritual substance. They were born from a movement of the Spirit but now have become a monument to His memory.
- Fasting tells God and your spiritual life: I'm serious about getting back to my spiritual life, being sensitive and available when following the Holy Spirit, and obeying His new direction, whatever it may be.

To demolish a fortress (aka religious monument) in our minds - for that precisely is what this is - sometimes we have to plunge into God's activities.

It's not enough to read some devotionals or make a few quick prayers; You have to demolish the fortresses that the enemy uses to keep you away from your next step in God.

This is a type of heart transplant. God has to remove from us something that is restricting our spiritual movements, a part that became unresponsive to His direction and to implant a new heart able to beat at the pace of His heart.

***He likes to hide because he loves
when we seek Him with all our hearts.***

Another example could be when you need to install a new engine in a car with a fused motor. You have to remove the old motor to replace it with a new one.

To do that, we must set apart our lives for God and give birth to that change in the depth of fasting and prayer.

As an example, think about Moses on the mount for forty days or Jesus in the wilderness for forty days. An encounter with God transformed them. Jacob (Genesis 32:25-32) left with a limp after he wrestled with the angel of God, but he received a new name: Israel. Now he relied on something different. He could no longer rely on his strength and needed to lean on a stick: God's strength.

Once we understand that the holy frustration, or lack of satisfaction in our hearts comes from the Holy Spirit, we can move into a position of seeking His guidance.

He likes to hide, because he loves it when we seek Him with all our hearts.

God did this so that they would seek him and perhaps reach out for him and find him, though he is not far from any one of us.
Acts 17:27

You will seek me and find me when you seek me with all your heart. I will be found by you," declares the Lord, "and will bring you back from captivity. I will gather you from all the nations and places where I have banished you," declares the Lord, "and will bring you back to the place from which I carried you into exile."
Jeremiah 29:13-14

2. LOOKING FOR
Looking for God in His Word.

During an intense fast, God has no doubt already begun to speak through hints, indications, sentences or images. Nevertheless, we don't always recognize them. That's when the Word starts to create clarity, confirm certain things, and open new roads. Ask the Holy Spirit: "from which book of the Bible do I start reading?"
Follow your first thought or image. If you think you're not getting a new instruction, start from the verses that you cherish or have received in the past. Meditate on the verses that blessed you or spoke to you in the past. By doing so, you can drink from a well that was in your life previously, but was closed and disused. Reopen those wells. Start from there.

> *Isaac reopened the wells that had been dug in the time of his father Abraham, which the Philistines had stopped up after Abraham died, and he gave them the same names his father had given them.*
> **Genesis 26:18**

Throughout my walk of faith, I often, if not always, noticed that some projects fail because they are based on earthly facts, numbers, and prerogatives - instead of on God's Word.

> *Keep this Book of the Law always on your lips; meditate on it day and night, so that you may be careful to do everything written in it. Then you will be prosperous and successful.*
> **Joshua 1:8**

In the above verse, the Hebrew word for "meditate" is HAGAH, which means: to meditate, dwell on, ruminate, conceive, design, imagine, draw, plan, murmur, mumble, whisper, utter, articulate, speak, growl, roar.

Simply put, to MEDITATE on the Word, means to carry your own words, thoughts and projects, the things God has shown you, into your time of reading the Word.

Not meditating on the Word will deprive us of some of the glorious things God has in store for us.

In my study time, I always use the three I's of biblical meditation:
1. immerse in the Word;
2. identify with the Word;
3. imagine the Word.

> *Meditate on it [...] Then you will be prosperous and successful.*
> **Joshua 1:8**

According to the promise we just read, if meditating on the Word empowers our lives, what happens when we meditate on something else?

NOT meditating on the Word will deprive us of some of the glorious things God has in store for us, things that will only activate when we allow the Word to break into our lives.

Only by meditating on what God says, can I then be positioned for success in my day while I work. *"Meditate [...] Then you will be prosperous and successful."*

Meditating revives the eyes of the heart.

Meditating and immersing myself in the Word, will give me access to revelation (removing the veil from minds) that will drive me to a new dimension (the depths of the Spirit where I'm already blessed with every spiritual blessing in Christ). It is in this place that I discover ways, resources, ideas, keys, instructions, connections, and much more. Things I couldn't even imagine would have existed, but God had them in store for my success.

The mere "knowing" the Word of God will not guarantee my success, but the revelation I'll receive about it through meditation will show me the step God wants me to take. My obedience to that divine instruction will take me where God has promised.

- To MEDITATE allows God to show you his heart through the Word for your projects, thoughts and plans.

By meditating on the Word, you will see God give you new "inputs" in your life. Meditating revives the eyes of the heart so that you are able to receive guidance throughout the day. You will start seeing and identifying concealed messages - specific indications that you couldn't see before: dreams, visions, messages, things you may even hear, that contain concealed messages to you.

Fasting and prayer, together with meditation, are reactivating your spiritual senses and enabling you to pick up these messages.

God will start showing you that He is with you, that there are steps to progression you can take. He will show you that He hasn't changed or forgotten you - indeed, He was waiting for you for a long time, right there where you left Him: in the Spirit, where your real identity comes from.

3. RESPONDING
Take any step God is showing you, big or small.

God can show you through prayer and fasting to even end a negative relationship or to start a new relationship. Once again, the wisest thing to do is to use the catalyst: fasting and prayer.

Ask God to confirm in your heart, then act. Even though not sensational, your first step of obedience will activate a domino effect in your spiritual life. You will experience and feel His presence more intensely than before. You will sense the Holy Spirit more distinctly and closer to you - and start to have concrete evidence of God's divine guidance in your life. Joy and peace are always the result of a step taken in agreement with the Holy Spirit. It will not necessarily be an exterior joy - it will be inner joy.

We need to learn to trust Him and not force the doors He has closed.

A holy dissatisfaction can be a spiritual indicator of something new God has in store for us. But we will not reach the new things God has for us if we are not willing to leave the old ones in God's hands. Therefore, we have to look intensely for the will of God by diligently withdrawing and spending time meditating on the Word. After having recognized His instructions and signs, we have to take each instruction one at a time as show by the Holy Spirit and take action.

The joy will be the sign that we have taken the right path - but we have to keep going.

Living with God doesn't mean taking a step once in a while; it's a continuous journey of faith. It's walking with the Holy Spirit - it's not occasionally visiting Him. It means to develop sensitivity not only to His voice but also to His heart, methods, ways, pace. We have to learn to trust Him and not force the doors He has closed.

When you have been living in a holy frustration a long time, you may have developed distrust towards God and His guidance. Not because He has abandoned us, but because we haven't understood His ways yet. We tried to force Him into our ways - but God's ways aren't ours.

> *As the heavens are higher than the earth, so are*
> *my ways higher than your ways and my thoughts*
> *than your thoughts.*
> **Isaiah 55:9**

God loves doing things His way, often through longer roads that do not make sense to us, even although we know that His ways will bring us to our destination.

My friends, if you have such an indicator in your hearts, it means that God is talking to you in this way.

NOTES

YOUR BODY SPEAKS TO YOU DAILY
THROUGH NEEDS, IMPULSES,
REQUESTS, AND PRIORITIES.
WE HAVE TO TAKE THEM INTO
ACCOUNT, BUT THEY MUST
NEVER GUIDE US.

- Francesco Basile

CHAPTER 12

FASTING MAKES ROOM FOR GOD

Fasting causes you to separate from everyday life to enter a specific time, set apart only for God, in which you prove by your actions how important He is to you: more important than food, your schedule, your friends. It's a time when you withdraw, consecrating a unique moment to God. It's not just for a few people, but for all who are guided by the Holy Spirit.

Through fasting, God wants to bring you back to look for a deeper intimacy with Him. He wants to remove all the things that are important to you. Fasting gets through your schedule, because God wants to have a significant encounter with you!

Fasting separates what is physical from what is spiritual, it makes a clean cut!

Your body speaks to you daily through needs, impulses, requests and priorities. We have to take them into account, but they must never guide us. People are led all the time by their senses, by what they see, touch, smell, hear and taste. On the other hand, believers are called to be led by the Holy Spirit (Romans 8:14).

From the beginning, God has created humans to be rulers and governors in His own image. God is Spirit, and his worshipers must worship in Spirit and truth. **We are spirit, soul and body**.

Paul calls the body *"a tent"*: *"The desire to break camp here and be with Christ is powerful,"* but you are not your body; you are a spiritual being living in a body.

God said to Jeremiah: *"Before I formed you in the womb, I knew you [...]"*, i.e., God knew him before Jeremiah had a physical body, because Jeremiah's real nature wasn't his body but his spiritual being. When we die, we leave our bodies, but we don't cease to exist. Jesus said: *"Father, into your hands I commit my spirit."* He didn't commit His body, but His Spirit. We are spiritual beings living in a body, and we have souls through which we interact with the outside world.

Humans in His image are spiritual, complex and powerful beings, but they would not have authority over the earth without a body: the **body** enables us to work on earth.

> *May God himself, the God of peace, sanctify you through and through. May your whole spirit, soul and body be kept blameless at the coming of our Lord Jesus Christ.*
> **1 Thessalonians 5:23**

In the beginning, humans were connected to heaven, they listened to God and did God's work. The, as a consequence of their sin, they started to be guided by their senses instead of God's Spirit. Scripture says: *"when you eat from it, you will certainly die."* Sin spiritually disconnected humans from the Creator. By examining the word "die" in the above context, we will find that it's not a matter of physical death. It's about spiritual death, namely separation from the spring of life. To start doing the things God has always wanted us to do, we must submit our feelings and bodily desires to our spirit - that, therefore, must return to rule.

When we truly experience the annihilation of our flesh and let God guide us to victory over this trial through the Word, the things God has stored in us will emerge. Prayer and fasting teach you how to connect onto the Holy Spirit so that we become a tool in God's hands.

When you fast, you're praying with your body.

Paul said: *"For if I pray in a tongue, my spirit prays, but my mind is unfruitful. So, what shall I do? I will pray with my spirit, but I will also pray with my understanding."*

When you pray in the heavenly language, you're praying with your Spirit; when you pray with your mind, you're praying with your soul; when you fast, you're praying with your body.

> *Love the Lord your God with all your heart and*
> *with all your soul and with all your mind and*
> *with all your strength.*
> **Mark 12:30**

Fasting lets every cell of your body pray!

Doctors have scientifically proven that one day of fasting per week helps with the regeneration of the body. This shows us that our body, organs, blood chemistry and everything within us, all start to understand that we are serious about God. Fasting has many benefits. Some sick people got well by taking a "fasting cure."

The disciples of Jesus used to fast. After having lost his sight on the way to Damascus, Saul didn't eat or drink anything for three days. Fasting is the highest form of prayer. When you fast, it will seem to you that your flesh is rebelling. You may feel weak, without strength, but you are getting spiritually stronger.

Some people might think that Paul was in crisis, but he was strengthening himself by praying and fasting instead. He recalled Moses and Samuel's story; he knew how they replied when the Lord called them. He knew well that God always appears with a purpose. That's why PAUL replied: *"What do you want me to do?"* The best thing you can do when God speaks to you is to start praying! Paul was serious about God.

The best thing you can do when you want to get out of a situation is prayer and fasting. Look for solutions from God, not from people! Let's see how good Jesus was when He appeared in a vision to Paul and said: *"Now get up and go into the city, and you will be told what you must do."*
Meanwhile, he appeared in a vision to Ananias too, telling him to lay hands on Paul so that Paul could regain his sight (Acts 9). When you obey God, He will tell someone else about you, to help you and give you what He promised to you!

There are several kinds of fasting, and the Scripture gives many examples, such as the one just mentioned; nevertheless, fasting is a personal thing. You have to find the more suitable combination between God and you - the one that works.

Nobody starts big, but one has to start to become big!
It's not easy to pray two or three hours a day from the very beginning, but you have to gradually develop a relationship with the

Lord that goes deeper than the surface. The more time passes, the more you'll get your spirit exercised in the things of God. You need to train yourself to fast. By developing a fasting discipline, you take your position on the throne of your spiritual life again.

Fasting tells your body that you are a united-with-God being and that He is in first place in your life.

Fasting and prayer are an explosive combination. The Lord spoke to me through a preacher once about intimacy with Him. The thing that deeply struck me was that the preacher said: *"Many people let their bodies have command over them all their lives, and then they complain when their bodies don't obey them in receiving healing!"*

Fasting gives you the power to take authority over your body; fasting doesn't change God, but it changes you; fasting doesn't make God move towards you, but makes your body move towards God and His power!

A man and a woman who pray make the darkness tremble because they have realized that they are **in** the world but are not **of** the world.

If you want to see a difference in your life, you have to listen to heaven, being one with heaven, go back to basics, as God created you, to listen to His voice, dominate, and rule!

Prayer and fasting annihilates my flesh and, as it loses strength, my body becomes more and more of a tool for God, not a tool of my own carnality.

When you fast, you sense a new dimension and feel that your body is more sensitive to the things of God, in particular to His power. Our bodies transmit God's power. When you fast, your body becomes a conductor of His power that permeates and takes authority over all your cells.

I often do extended fasting, and every time I pray for someone, an unusual power flows through my body - one that I rarely experience without fasting. I assure you that if you do what has been spoken about through this book, you'll be able to experience the SUPERNATURAL POWER OF GOD in your life!

Fasting gives you the power to take authority over your body; fasting doesn't change God, but it changes you; fasting doesn't make God move towards you, but makes your body move towards God and His power!

NOTES

Conclusion

Thanks for making it to the end! Now that we know each other a little better you will have understood, in the pages of my book, that writing is just one of the things that God has given me the grace to do to help others get to know him and follow his plan. When I started my studies way back in 1999 in Denmark, I immediately fell in love with Biblical training. Then in the years that have followed that course of study, especially studying in the USA at Victory Bible College, and in many other places in the world as I have already mentioned to you; I had the opportunity to learn how to transmit to others in a fast, practical and effective way those Biblical and spiritual principles that first of all transformed me and my family, but which I know by the grace of God, can transform anyone who has the desire to become mold from the Word of God. This is to tell you that on my return to Italy, after studying at university level at the feet of men of God of international caliber such as T.L. Osborn, Billy Joe Daugherty, Myles Monroe, John Maxwell and many others, I have been recognized by Victory as director of the Biblical Training School for Italy. Many people always have the price they will pay to pay for doing God's will, but not the price they will pay. God has only the best for our life, but every man or woman that God has used has always been prepared first.

Now lets stay in touch, and discover all Francesco's material simply going on our web: www.francescobasile.tv

francescobasile.tv

NOTES

NOTES

NOTES

NOTES

NOTES

NOTES

NOTES

NOTES

NOTES

NOTES

NOTES

NOTES

NOTES

NOTES

NOTES

NOTES

Printed in Poland
by Amazon Fulfillment
Poland Sp. z o.o., Wrocław

23037631R00069